THE MOTHER

A Collection of Poems Written by a
Mother for All The Mothers

Lizzie Fairless

Contents

The First Time I Held Her 1

She Is Already Whole 3

Utter Joy 5

What Will She Be? 7

When You Test Me 9

Run To Me 11

Tiny Steps 13

The Loyal Friend 15

When You Fall In Love 17

The Explorer 19

Take My Body 21

I Am Your Mother 23

The World Is On Fire 25

Bed Time 27

Spring 29

The Weight 31

It Gets Harder 33

For Story, my little wildling.

The First Time I Held Her

He handed her to me,
and she immediately felt like the heaviest thing I had ever held.
I could see how tiny her feet were,
the fluid around her eyes formed in the shape of a teardrop,
and even in that moment of pure joy,
I felt a slight and sudden sadness in remembering that one day,
she too, would feel the pains of being human.

She Is Already Whole

Heavy and light, all at once.
A balance of friendship and hard boundaries,
leading with confidence (newfound),
completely aware that every little thing I do and say matters so
much in some ways,
and not at all in others.
Completely in touch with how these moments will mold her into
the daughter, friend, and lover she will one day become.
I do this job with serious intention,
so that she may lead with kindness but stand firm in who she is;
so much so, that she can give love in the healthiest ways
because she is already whole.

Utter Joy

I knew what it would feel like,
I thought.
But it was so much more delicate than I could have imagined.
A dance of happiness, shadowed by mourning.
Each day is new, and so are they.
And then it is gone, and so are they,
different than they were the day before.
It is all so magical and fleeting,
I want to bottle it up and let it fly with abundance,
because it is all so
beautiful to me,
and I'd like to remember it.

What Will She Be?

I try so hard not to imagine.
I try so hard not to project
any notion of my own onto who this little wilding will become.
I fantasize quietly about all the good she will do.
I remind myself never to put that pressure on her, out loud.
I walk myself through the knowing that she may do absolutely
nothing with this gift I have given her.
But she will still be spectacular,
because spectacular is in her bones.

When You Test Me

When you test me,
I try to remember all of the times I dreamt of having a daughter
that would test me.
I think of all the times I wept in fear,
Big and pregnant with you in my belly.
I was so afraid that I would never meet you.
But here you are,
bold and brave.
Oh, how you test me.
And teach me.
You have been the greatest teacher,
the one who showed me the universe was in being mother.

Run To Me

Half this job is following you.
Shadowing you through exploration,
you discover the world with me close behind.
Sometimes you speed up and fall over.
Quickly you stand up and look behind for me.
There I am.
You run to me.

Tiny Steps

If you want to be inspired,
if you want to complete your goals,
just look at your little one
taking all those tiny steps towards freedom.
Tiny steps lead to big milestones.
If only, as adults, we weren't so discouraged by tiny wins.
The tiny wins make for big accomplishments.

The Loyal Friend

Today I read that to find a loyal friend,
you must be a loyal friend, and rightly so.
I have never fared well in friendships.
They came before my internal revolution and never stayed to see
    the prize.
But with you my little wildling,
I would wage war to show my loyalty.
But we know now through countless lessons
learned through pain, and sometimes agony,
that going to war is not an act of love.
Love is in small, practiced actions,
    it's in keeping a calm head and cool tongue.
Loyalty is repetition.
It is showing up, not sometimes but always.
In every way.

When You Fall In Love

One day you will fall in love with someone.
I hope when this day comes you know exactly what you stand for.
The right person will not make you change this foundation.
The right person will not make you question your integrity, or your
state of mind.
They will meet you right where you are, little wildling,
and through love and compassion, you will grow
into two individuals, better for knowing one another.
But you must discover yourself first.
And I hope you spend your days writing your story,
the one you are named for.
I hope you discover a deep sense of self.
When you are steady in this idea,
That is when I hope you fall in love --
because you have done the work
to show up authentically yourself,
because you know no other way to be.

The Explorer

She sways from side to side.
With every step
so unsteady but so sure,
each foot planted in purpose,
a smile perched across her face.
The ground is always moving,
and so is she.
Fearless in her pursuit of conquering new territory.
She will have discovered and claimed
every inch of this place.
She is the explorer.

Take My Body

Your body will change, they tell you.
Your little breasts will grow big and round,
not in the way you'd like them to.
Once full, they'll nourish your wildling.
But then they will soon be empty
and they will droop
and smile at you in the mirror.
And you will remember your
happy, perky, small little breasts
that fed no one.

I Am Your Mother

I am your mother.
I am your fate.
I feed you
and love you
and nourish you.
Oh, how you nourish me.
Oh, how you've led me to healing.
I've been troubled, my sweet girl.
I've lived and loved.
I've faltered; you will, too.
But it led me to you,
my sweet one.
I am your mother,
and I am a daughter.
I am a sister.
One day you may be all those things, too.
Whatever you are,
you will always be my daughter.
I am your mother.
And I love you,
no matter what you do.

The World Is on Fire

It is hard to find comfort in the future with the whole world ablaze.
When I search for the picture of what her world will look like
20, 30, 40 years down the line
I am admittedly unsure of what I see.
So much has changed already in my lifespan, and fires seem to be
more frequent these days.
I brought her into this world, and I feel responsible for what she will
inherit.
I know that by teaching our children with compassion, instead of
fear, we are breaking generations-long trauma.
In doing so we are creating more well-equipped humans to take
care of what's left.
We can plant trees and ideas and guide them, but eventually
it will be in their hands.
All these fires will be theirs to put out.

Bed Time

Wide sleepy eyes,
the sweetest mouth, little lips red with youth.
Signs of a diaper sticking out from her jammies.
A loud shriek! A deep sigh. A silly giggle.
A book about sheep.
Will sheep sleep?
"NO!" she wails.
The heat on, just so.
The shades drawn.
The blanket spread.
Pandy perched.
A blessing read.
The switch of a light,
a kiss goodnight.

<u>**Spring**</u>

Spring taps its fingers on our window.
I can see that your tiny hands are growing strong.
We have watched the seasons cycle twice now
in this little house we've made a home.
I can see the decaying leaves turn over into new life.
I can see the subtle signs
that soon the animals will return,
and this time you will know them.
We will name them and watch them come and go.

The Weight

It is amazing how you love me.
You just woke up from a nap in tears,
and I held out my arms and you stopped crying.
Sometimes that power feels heavy; it can feel like a lot to carry.
But it feels like my life's purpose is to grow alongside you,
to show you through doing that every single thing is possible.
I remind myself that days off are necessary,
to give myself grace as "Rome was not built in a day,"
and a person needs rest to recharge and reset.
I would want you to take a rest if you needed it.
Dreams are hard to chase, but not impossible if, while chasing,
    you recognize that you are already remarkable for trying.

It Gets Harder

People keep telling me that "it gets harder when they get older."
But it has always been hard.
I still take you everywhere,
because I want you to be everywhere with me.
I want you to see everything.
I want you to feel like you lived every day,
because you deserve to know every ounce of what this world has
to offer.
I keep you safe, but I let you dream.
I make sure you're close, but I let you wonder.
I romanticize your every step,
because I hope
that one day you will come to romanticize them, too.
It's always been hard, but easy doesn't make for great stories.
And you were taught that on the other side of hard
is everything you ever wanted.